MIGHTY MACHINES

by Maureen Spurgeon　　　　*illustrated by Brian Bartle*

Brown Watson

ENGLAND

This edition first published 2004 by
Brown Watson
The Old Mill, 76 Fleckney Road,
Kibworth Beauchamp, Leicestershire LE8 0HG

© 1995 Brown Watson, England

Printed in Belgium

ISBN: 0-7097-1631-1

CONTENTS

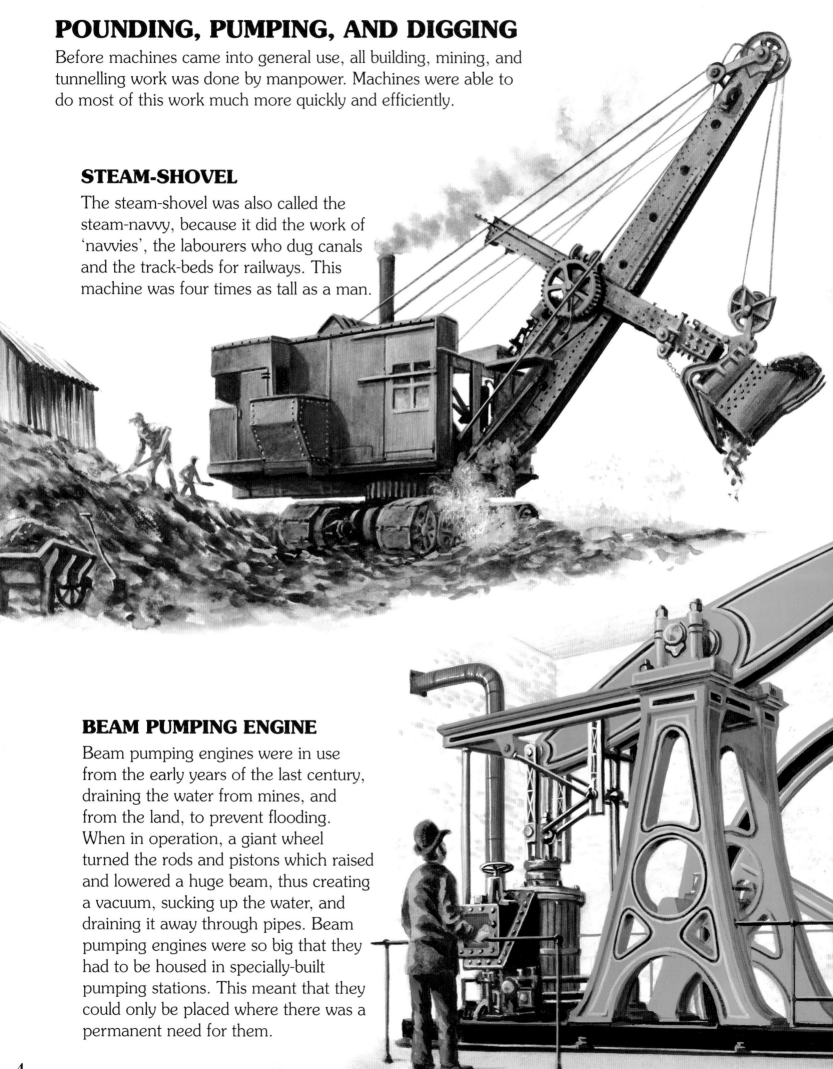

POUNDING, PUMPING, AND DIGGING

Before machines came into general use, all building, mining, and tunnelling work was done by manpower. Machines were able to do most of this work much more quickly and efficiently.

STEAM-SHOVEL

The steam-shovel was also called the steam-navvy, because it did the work of 'navvies', the labourers who dug canals and the track-beds for railways. This machine was four times as tall as a man.

BEAM PUMPING ENGINE

Beam pumping engines were in use from the early years of the last century, draining the water from mines, and from the land, to prevent flooding. When in operation, a giant wheel turned the rods and pistons which raised and lowered a huge beam, thus creating a vacuum, sucking up the water, and draining it away through pipes. Beam pumping engines were so big that they had to be housed in specially-built pumping stations. This meant that they could only be placed where there was a permanent need for them.

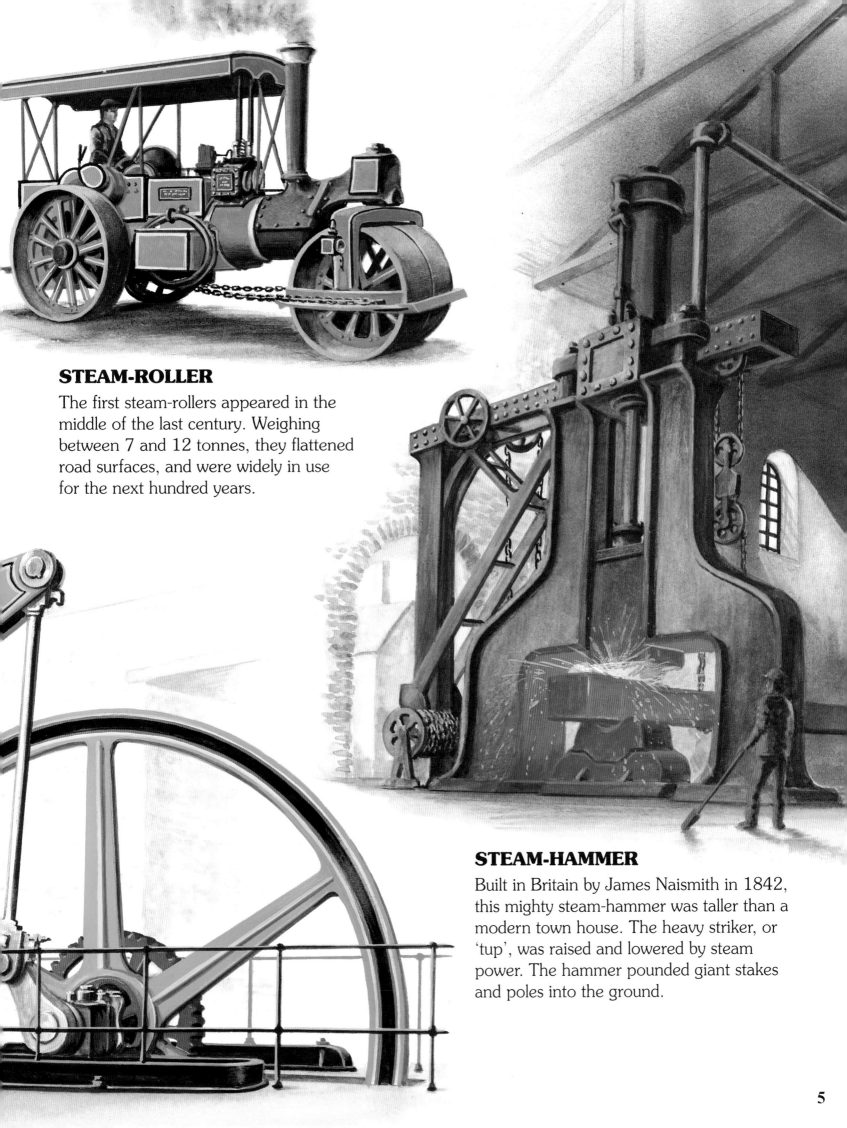

STEAM-ROLLER

The first steam-rollers appeared in the middle of the last century. Weighing between 7 and 12 tonnes, they flattened road surfaces, and were widely in use for the next hundred years.

STEAM-HAMMER

Built in Britain by James Naismith in 1842, this mighty steam-hammer was taller than a modern town house. The heavy striker, or 'tup', was raised and lowered by steam power. The hammer pounded giant stakes and poles into the ground.

TRACTORS AND TOOLS

Although farmers understood how much time a tractor could save them, and what work it could do for them, for a very long time, even after manufacturers started making them, a tractor was too expensive for a farmer to purchase. Horses remained the most common form of power on a farm up until the late 1930s. By then, a whole range of new tools had been developed for use with a tractor, so that it was able to do even more work for its owner.

PLOUGH

At first, tractor-pulled ploughs could only dig one or two furrows at a time. Now, six or more furrows can be ploughed simultaneously.

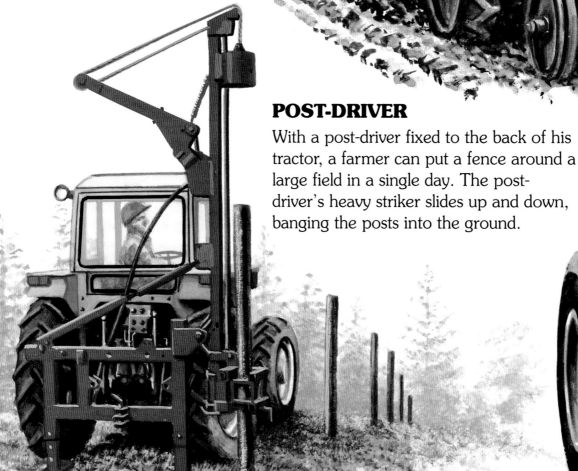

POST-DRIVER

With a post-driver fixed to the back of his tractor, a farmer can put a fence around a large field in a single day. The post-driver's heavy striker slides up and down, banging the posts into the ground.

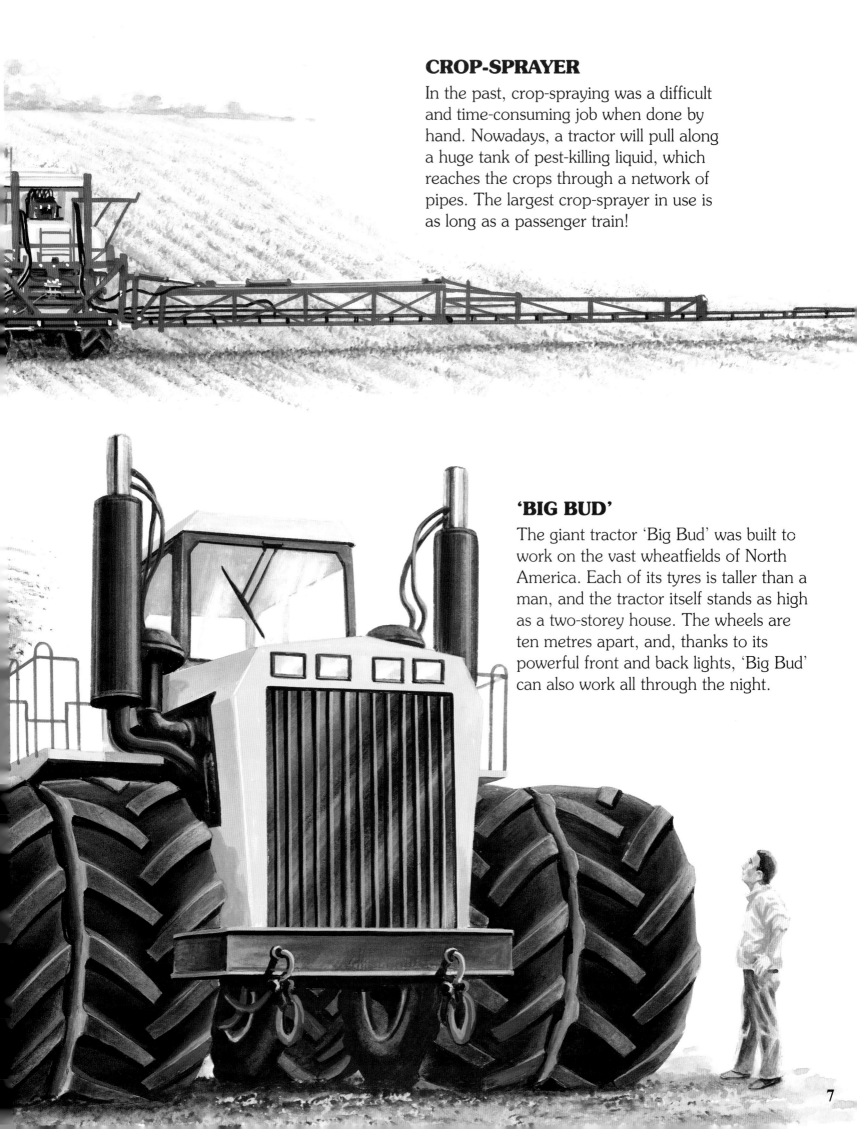

CROP-SPRAYER

In the past, crop-spraying was a difficult and time-consuming job when done by hand. Nowadays, a tractor will pull along a huge tank of pest-killing liquid, which reaches the crops through a network of pipes. The largest crop-sprayer in use is as long as a passenger train!

'BIG BUD'

The giant tractor 'Big Bud' was built to work on the vast wheatfields of North America. Each of its tyres is taller than a man, and the tractor itself stands as high as a two-storey house. The wheels are ten metres apart, and, thanks to its powerful front and back lights, 'Big Bud' can also work all through the night.

HARVESTING BY MACHINE

The harvest is the end-result of a whole year's hard work by the farmer . . . and everything can be spoiled by even a short spell of bad weather at harvest-time. Speed is essential when the crops are being brought in. Through the use of machinery, the work of harvesting can be done in much less time than when the job had to be done by human labour alone.

BIG-BALER

When the combine harvester has cut down the crop, the big-baler gathers up the straw that remains, and rolls it, or bundles it, into huge bales. Each bale weighs as much as eight men.

ROOT-CROP HARVESTER

Root-crops, such as potatoes, carrots, onions, or turnips, are dug up by the root-crop harvester. The machine then strips off the leaves, takes the vegetables up a small elevator, and tips them on to a moving belt. There is room on the machine for a team of pickers to stand beside this belt, taking out any bad or damaged produce, before the rest of the crop goes into a separate trailer.

COMBINE HARVESTER

The first combine harvesters were drawn by tractors. Now, a combine harvester is a machine in its own right. After it has cut and then threshed the crop, the grain is poured out into a lorry or other container. Giant combine harvesters can produce up to 15 tonnes of grain per hour.

9

EXCAVATORS AND EARTH-MOVERS

Excavators and earth-movers are machines which dig and move earth. Some of these machines are used for digging the foundations of buildings or roads, and others dig deep trenches and tunnels.

BACKHOE LOADER

This machine has a bucket at the back, and a loader, or loading shovel, at the front. The largest of these machines is twice the height of a man, and as long as a football pitch!

BACKHOE EXCAVATOR

The vast metal bucket of a backhoe excavator can dig out up to 1.5 tonnes of earth at a time . . . more than the combined weight of 18 men!

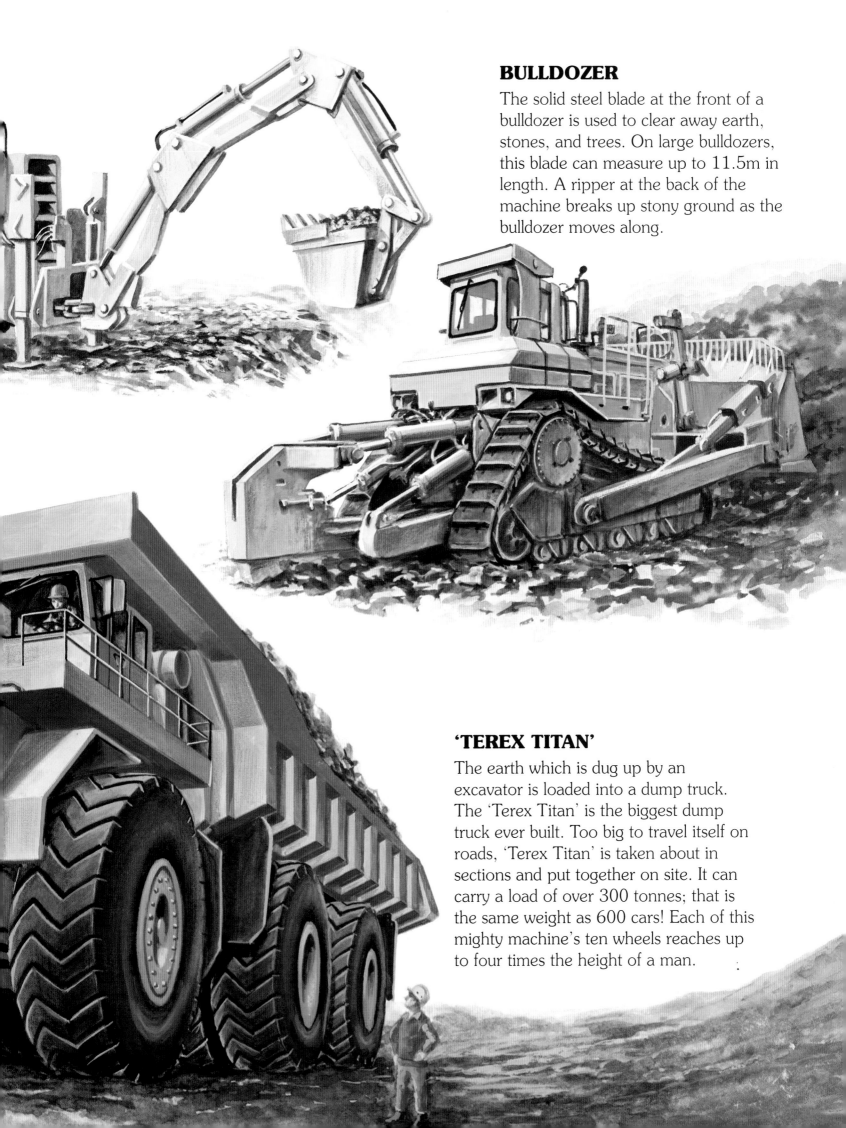

BULLDOZER

The solid steel blade at the front of a bulldozer is used to clear away earth, stones, and trees. On large bulldozers, this blade can measure up to 11.5m in length. A ripper at the back of the machine breaks up stony ground as the bulldozer moves along.

'TEREX TITAN'

The earth which is dug up by an excavator is loaded into a dump truck. The 'Terex Titan' is the biggest dump truck ever built. Too big to travel itself on roads, 'Terex Titan' is taken about in sections and put together on site. It can carry a load of over 300 tonnes; that is the same weight as 600 cars! Each of this mighty machine's ten wheels reaches up to four times the height of a man.

TRAVELLING CRANES

Travelling cranes have wheels, and they 'travel' along tracks or rails, taking loads from one place to another. The rails along which they move can be on the ground or overhead, outdoors or in.

CONTAINER CRANE

Container cranes are mostly seen on the quaysides in harbours, loading and unloading containers on and off ships. The average height of one of these cranes is 60m, and their length 80m.

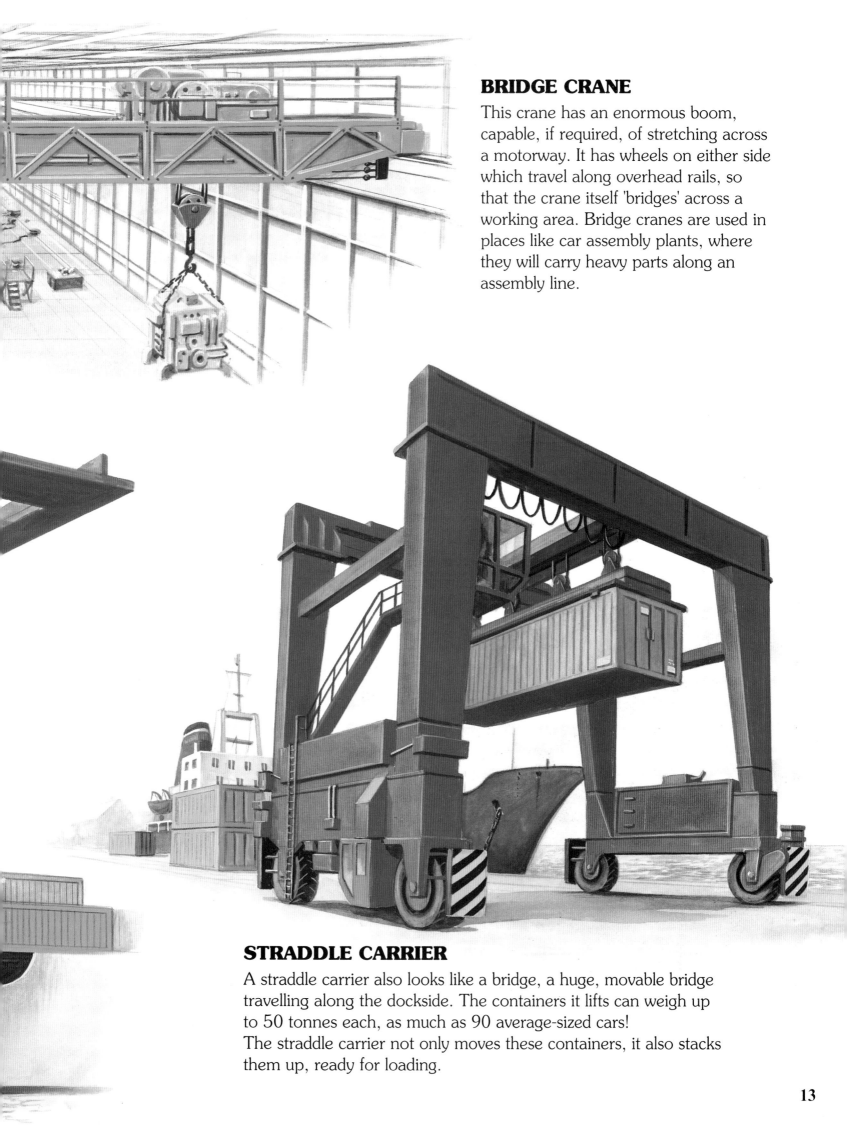

BRIDGE CRANE

This crane has an enormous boom, capable, if required, of stretching across a motorway. It has wheels on either side which travel along overhead rails, so that the crane itself 'bridges' across a working area. Bridge cranes are used in places like car assembly plants, where they will carry heavy parts along an assembly line.

STRADDLE CARRIER

A straddle carrier also looks like a bridge, a huge, movable bridge travelling along the dockside. The containers it lifts can weigh up to 50 tonnes each, as much as 90 average-sized cars!
The straddle carrier not only moves these containers, it also stacks them up, ready for loading.

MACHINES FOR BUILDING WORK

As the average height of buildings in large towns becomes greater, so the machines used in constructing them have to be larger and stronger. Some of the biggest of these machines are used in the building of high-rise apartments and office blocks.

TOWER CRANE

A tower crane arrives at a building site in sections. As the new building grows in height, additional sections are added to the tower crane, and bolted on. The tower crane's boom can be almost as long as a soccer pitch.

CONCRETE MIXER

The stone, sand, and cement which make up concrete are mixed in the drum as the concrete mixer is being driven to the building site. The drum is so large that you could fit a car inside it.

CONCRETE PUMP

This machine sucks up concrete from a big tank or hopper at the back, then pumps it out through a pipe that is 23m long . . . more than the length of three buses.

DROP-HAMMER CRANE

The task of the drop-hammer crane is to drive steel piles into the ground when the foundations of buildings are being laid. The hammer, which weighs up to 8 tonnes, is dropped from a height of up to 80cm.

AUGER CRANE

'Auger' is the name for a large screw or drill, and the auger crane is often called the 'drilling crane.' The auger, which is fixed to the top of the crane's boom, is as tall as a high-rise block of flats.

CRANES AT SEA

Huge floating cranes load and unload ships when there are no travelling cranes available to do the work. Other sea-going cranes are used for building deep-sea oil or gas rigs. These cranes are among the largest that have been made.

FLOATING CRANE

A floating crane is built on a pontoon, or floating platform. Heavy ropes link the pontoon to the edge of the quay until the loading or unloading of a cargo ship has been completed. The largest of these floating cranes can be three times as high as a house.

SEMI-SUBMERSIBLE CRANE VESSEL

'Semi-submersible' means partly underwater. This giant machine sails from one job to another. It has a crawler crane which moves around its 154m-long deck, as well as two enormous cranes that work together to lift whole sections of oil rigs and gas platforms into position. Each crane can lift up to 1,000 tonnes . . . as much as the weight of a ship! Over 300 men live and work on the crane vessel for months at a time.

17

ROAD-BUILDING MACHINES

Ancient civilisations built roads with layers of gravel, sand, and stone. Our modern roads are built in much the same way, except that, on top, there are layers of hot tarmac, or asphalt, which consists of hot tar and small stones mixed together.

GRADER

A grader has a heavy steel blade which smooths a bottom layer of stones over the ground. Its blade is over 4m long.

SCRAPER

A scraper is over 7m long. It levels the ground, cutting down all the lumps and bumps with sharp metal plates mounted on a belt which moves round as the machine goes along. The earth that is scraped loose is then gathered in a big metal box.

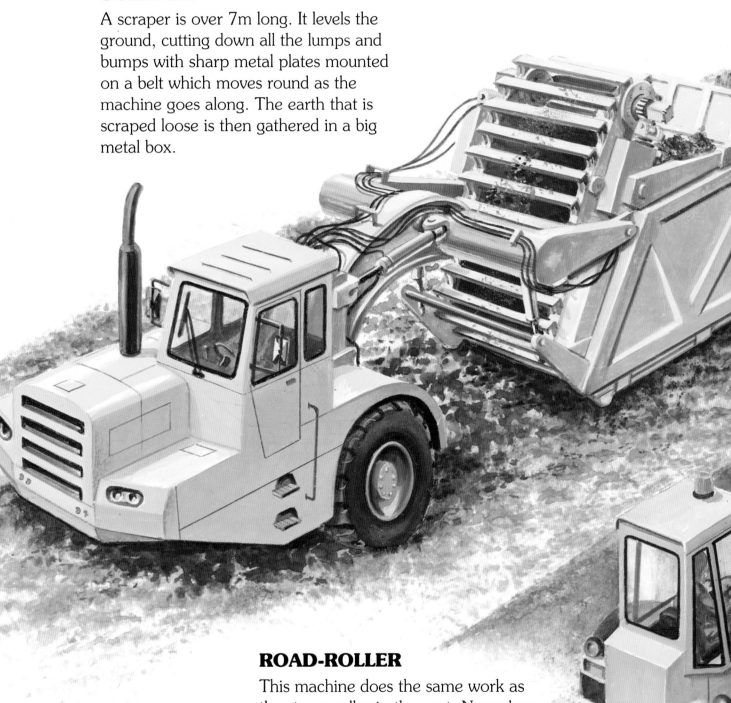

ROAD-ROLLER

This machine does the same work as the steam-roller in the past. Nowadays, the roller wheels are hollow steel, filled with sand or water, making them even heavier than the solid steel wheels of the old steam-roller.

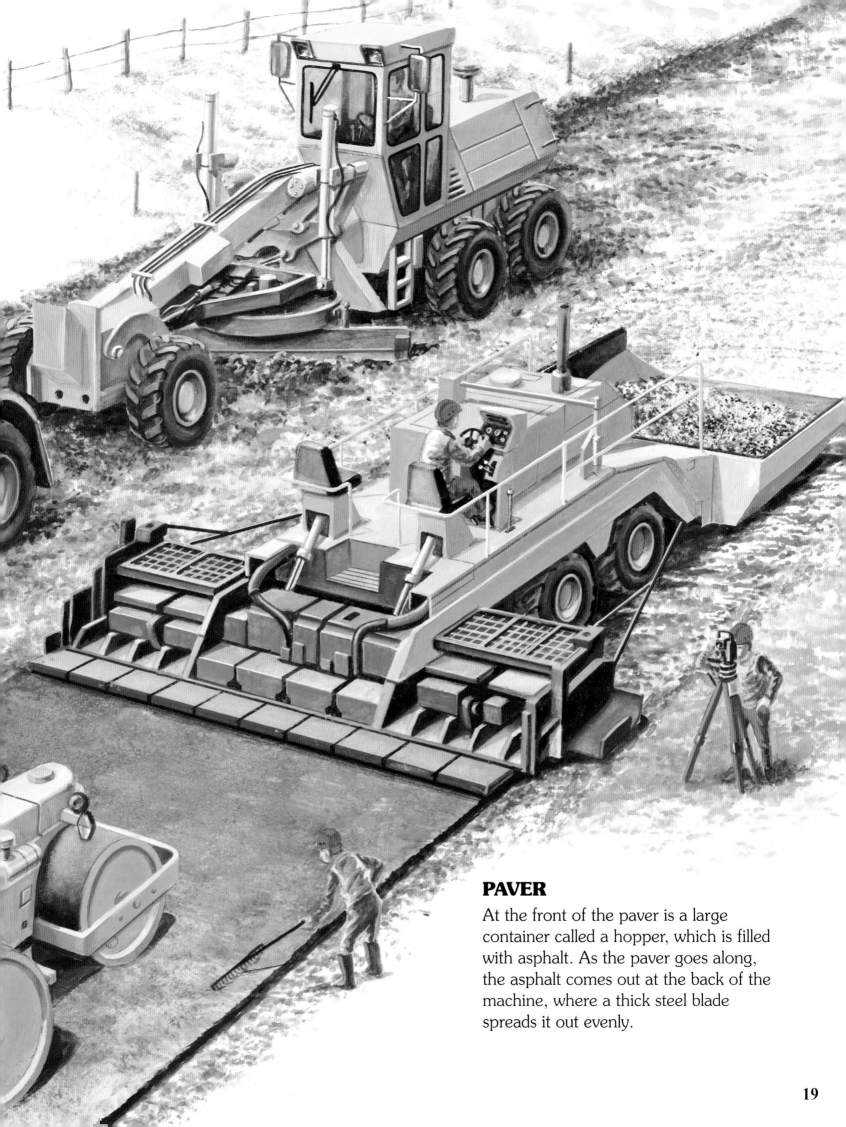

PAVER

At the front of the paver is a large container called a hopper, which is filled with asphalt. As the paver goes along, the asphalt comes out at the back of the machine, where a thick steel blade spreads it out evenly.

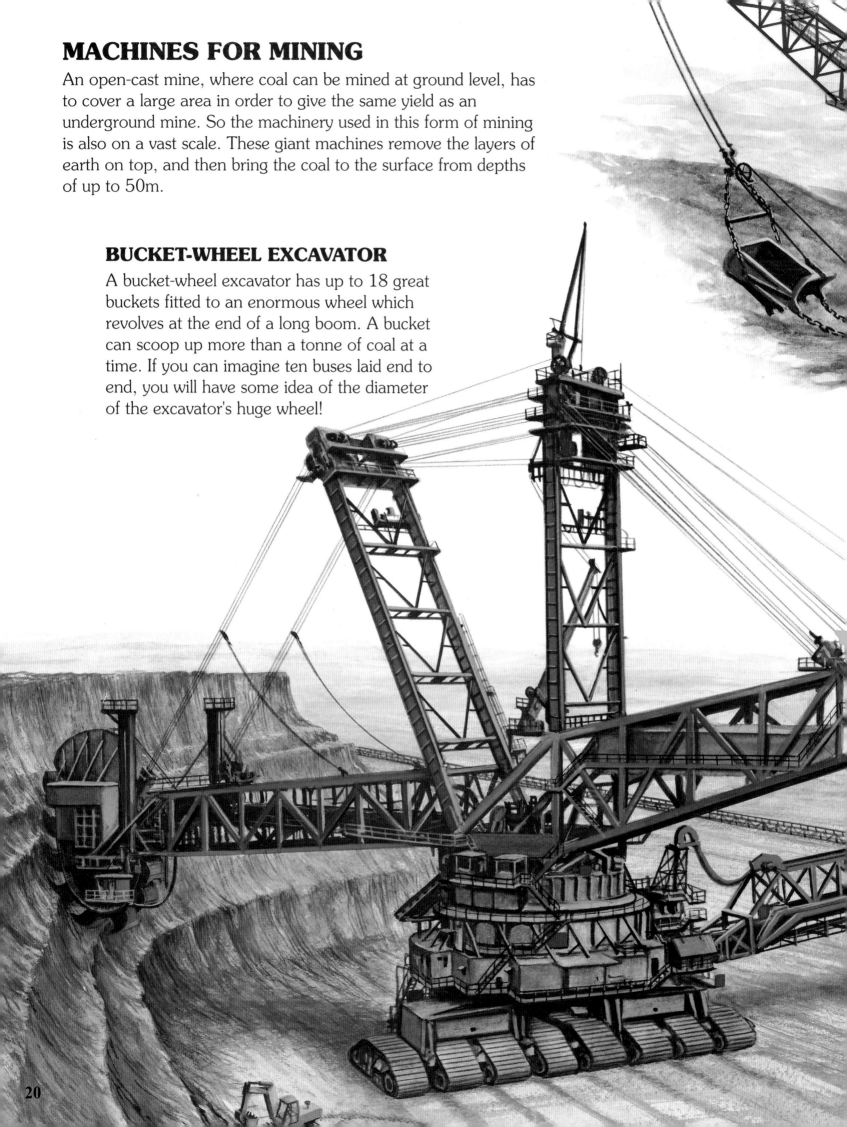

MACHINES FOR MINING

An open-cast mine, where coal can be mined at ground level, has to cover a large area in order to give the same yield as an underground mine. So the machinery used in this form of mining is also on a vast scale. These giant machines remove the layers of earth on top, and then bring the coal to the surface from depths of up to 50m.

BUCKET-WHEEL EXCAVATOR

A bucket-wheel excavator has up to 18 great buckets fitted to an enormous wheel which revolves at the end of a long boom. A bucket can scoop up more than a tonne of coal at a time. If you can imagine ten buses laid end to end, you will have some idea of the diameter of the excavator's huge wheel!

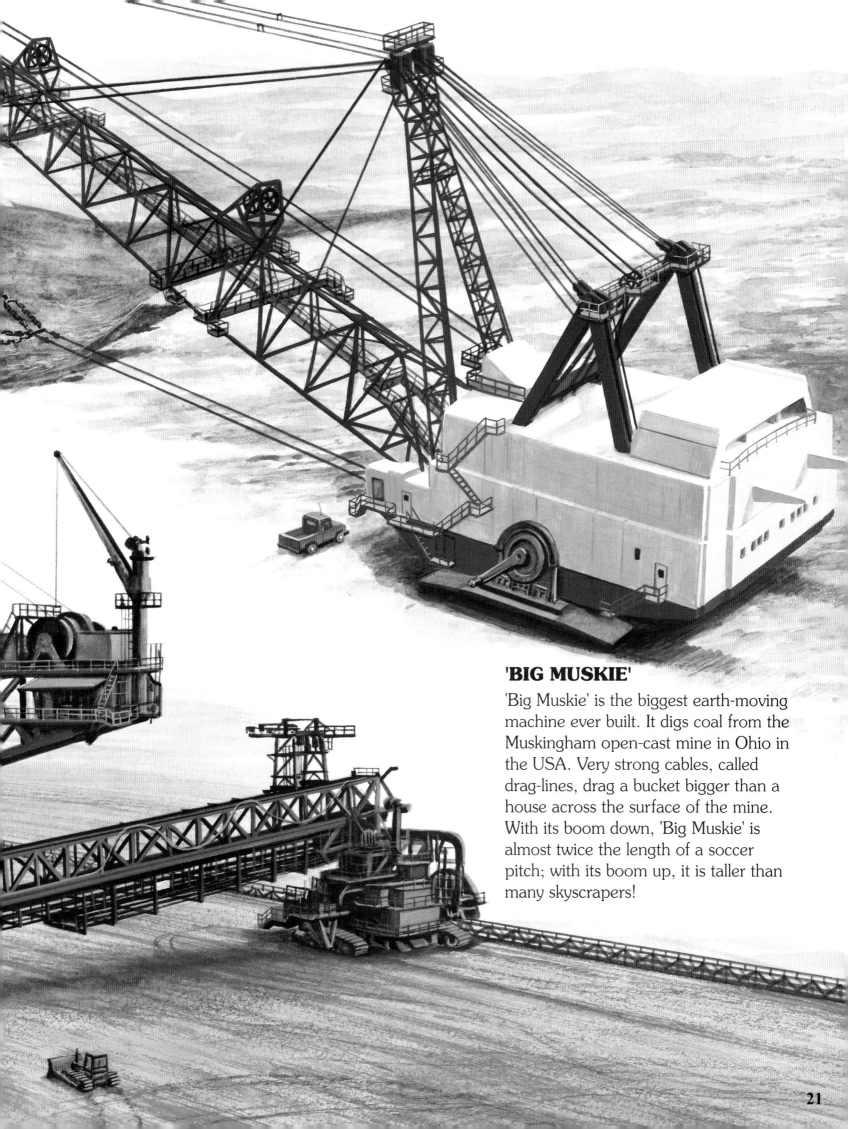

'BIG MUSKIE'

'Big Muskie' is the biggest earth-moving
machine ever built. It digs coal from the
Muskingham open-cast mine in Ohio in
the USA. Very strong cables, called
drag-lines, drag a bucket bigger than a
house across the surface of the mine.
With its boom down, 'Big Muskie' is
almost twice the length of a soccer
pitch; with its boom up, it is taller than
many skyscrapers!

UNDERGROUND GIANTS

Until little more than 120 years ago, all underground mining was done by men using picks and shovels. It was manpower and explosives that bored the road and railway tunnels out of the earth. Then machines began to be used.

ROAD-HEADER

Small tunnels called 'headings' are dug by the road-header. This machine has a cup-shaped head, covered with steel blades, which spins round to cut through solid rock. A road header weighs 42 tonnes, or to put it another way, five times the weight of a big fire engine! It is also 10m high, and 9m long.

TUNNEL-BORING MACHINES

At around 270m long, tunnel-boring machines, or TBMs, are the biggest tunnelling machines in the world. As the head of the machine bores its way forward, concrete sections are carried along a conveyor belt to an erector which lines the inside of the tunnel with them. A TBM can dig through over 6m of earth in an hour, cutting a tunnel which can be up to 10m in diameter.

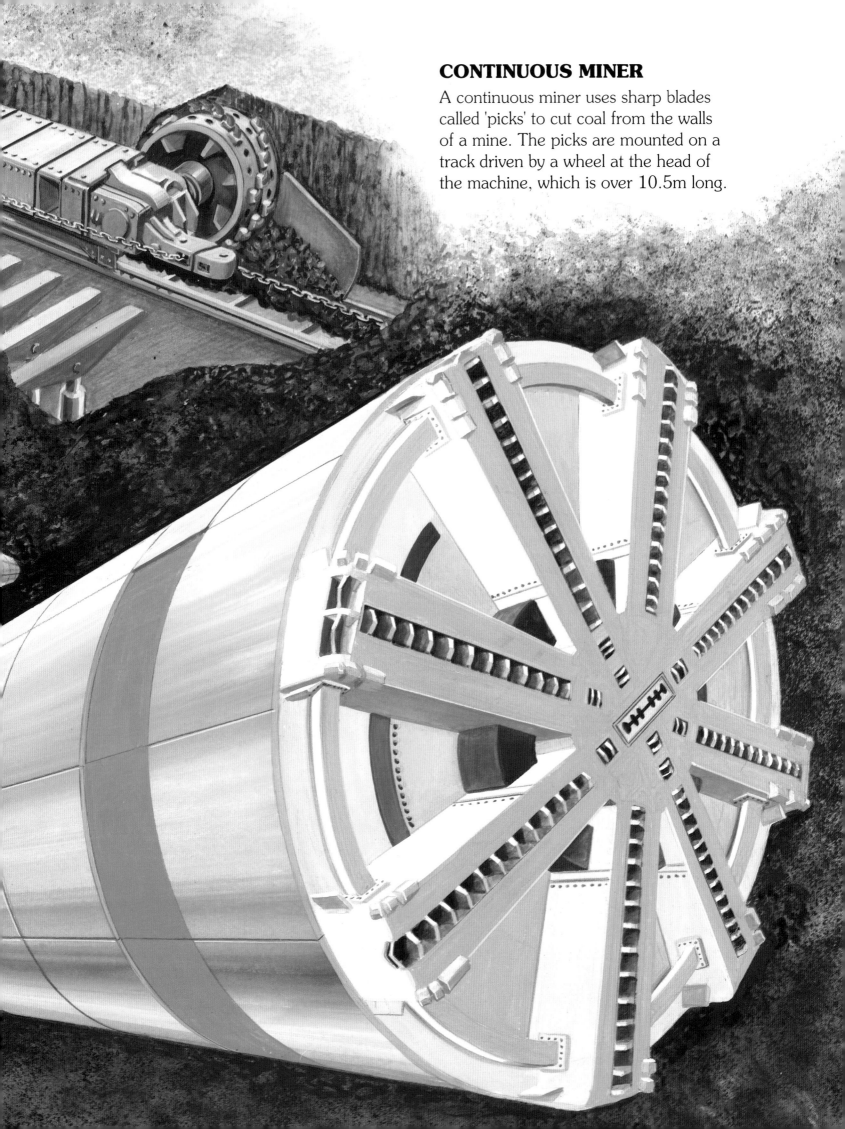

CONTINUOUS MINER

A continuous miner uses sharp blades called 'picks' to cut coal from the walls of a mine. The picks are mounted on a track driven by a wheel at the head of the machine, which is over 10.5m long.

GIANTS OF THE AIR

The quickest form of transportation is by air, both for passengers and cargo. With more and more people wanting to reach far-distant destinations speedily, and more and more supplies having to be delivered urgently to faraway parts of the world in emergency situations, ever bigger and more powerful aircraft have had to be constructed to meet these demands.

JUMBO JET - THE BOEING 747

This jet is the world's largest passenger airliner, capable of seating over 650 people on its two decks. It has a wingspan of nearly 60m, and it is over 70m in length; so it sits on an area about three times the size of a tennis court!

CONCORDE

Concorde was the world's first supersonic airliner, with a wingspan of nearly 29m and built to fly at twice the speed of sound – over 2,300 km/h! It was in passenger service from 1976 until October 2003.

THE US LOCKHEED C-58 GALAXY

This mighty aircraft can carry up to 370 troops, and, when its large, hinged nose is raised, 14 tanks can be driven into the massive cargo bay, which is over 40m long, and 6m wide. The Galaxy has a wingspan of over 67m, which is wider than a soccer pitch. On the runway, the aircraft rests on 28 enormous wheels.

THE WORLD'S LARGEST HELICOPTER

The Russian-built 'Mil-12 Homer' weighs over 100 tonnes, and is able to lift nearly 40 tonnes in weight at a time. It has a span of no less than 67m across its rotor tips.

MIGHTY MACHINES OF THE SEA

The biggest vessels on the sea are among the largest machines man has ever made.

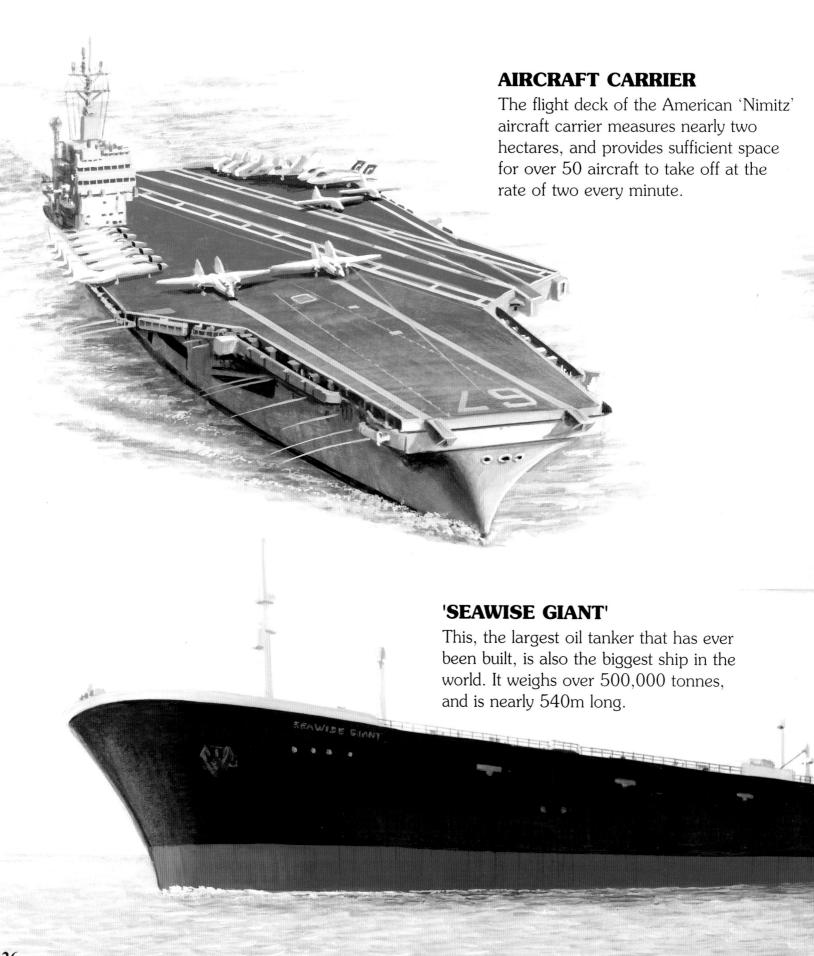

AIRCRAFT CARRIER

The flight deck of the American 'Nimitz' aircraft carrier measures nearly two hectares, and provides sufficient space for over 50 aircraft to take off at the rate of two every minute.

'SEAWISE GIANT'

This, the largest oil tanker that has ever been built, is also the biggest ship in the world. It weighs over 500,000 tonnes, and is nearly 540m long.

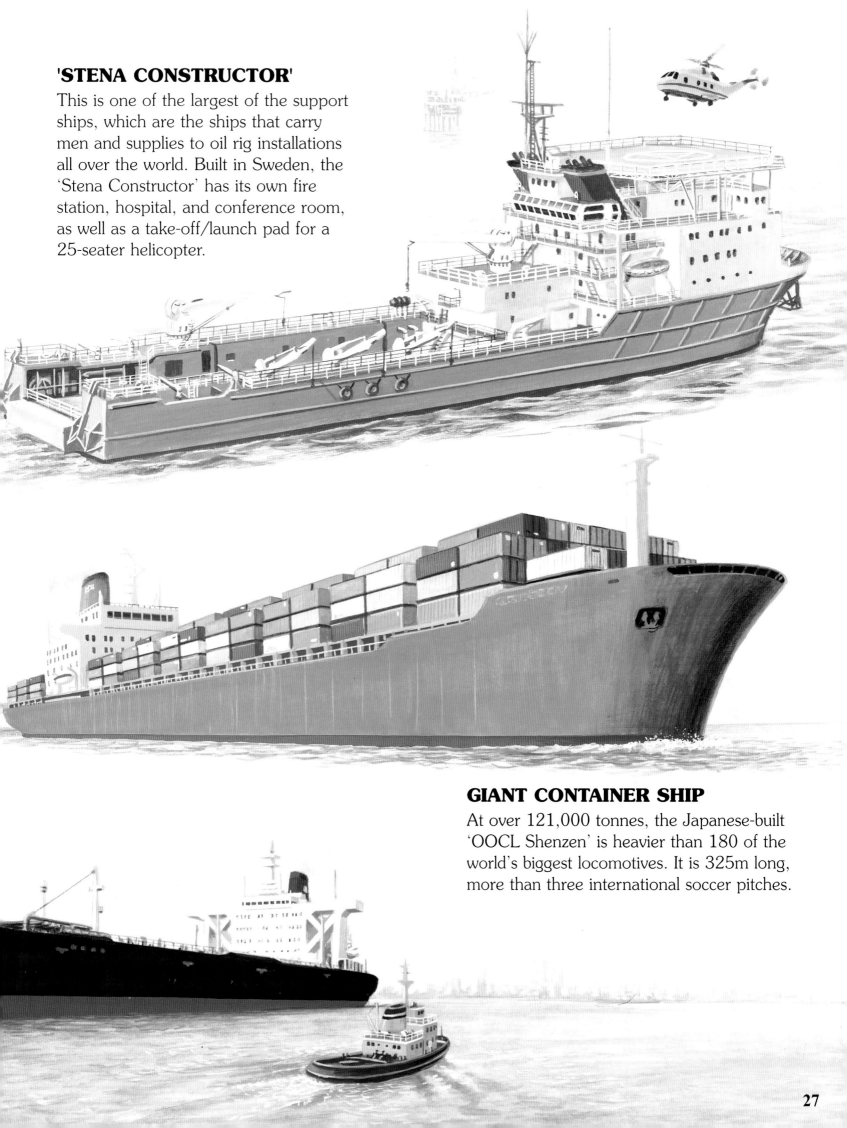

'STENA CONSTRUCTOR'

This is one of the largest of the support ships, which are the ships that carry men and supplies to oil rig installations all over the world. Built in Sweden, the 'Stena Constructor' has its own fire station, hospital, and conference room, as well as a take-off/launch pad for a 25-seater helicopter.

GIANT CONTAINER SHIP

At over 121,000 tonnes, the Japanese-built 'OOCL Shenzen' is heavier than 180 of the world's biggest locomotives. It is 325m long, more than three international soccer pitches.

GIANT LOCOMOTIVES

The first locomotives were steam-driven. Then came the diesel-powered locomotives, and finally today's modern electric locomotives. No matter what the type of locomotive, the main requirement has always been that they should have the strength and power to haul heavy trains over long distances.

'BIG BOY'

The Union Pacific locomotive 'Big Boy' is believed to be the largest ever built. It is 40.5m long, and weighs over 350 tonnes. Its main wheels are taller than a man, and, at 2.74m, the diameter of its boiler is greater than the width of today's biggest lorry.

UNION PACIFIC LOCOMOTIVES

The biggest diesel locomotives were two which belonged to the Union Pacific Railroad in the USA. Each of them weighed over 426 tonnes. Working together, these two mighty machines could move a train that was nearly 5km long!

T.G.V.

The initials 'T.G.V.' stand for the French words 'Train à Grande Vitesse' . . . meaning 'very fast train'. This train holds the world rail speed record at over 515km/h. The electric locomotive that pulls the T.G.V. is not only the fastest in the world today, but, at 22.15m long, it is also the largest.

MIGHTY MACHINES IN SPACE

Massive strength is required to overcome the pull of the Earth's gravity. Consequently, machines built for space exploration are some of the most powerful that man has ever made.

SPACE SHUTTLE

The US Space Shuttle makes return journeys into space, rather like a 'space bus'! The shuttle is launched by two great booster rockets, each over 110m tall. From base to nose cone, the shuttle's height is nearly 77m.

HUBBLE SPACE TELESCOPE

This is a joint US-European space project, the first man-made satellite orbiting the Earth that is serviced by the space shuttle. The Hubble telescope can see stars which are 50 times *fainter* than those that can be viewed by the largest ground-based telescopes, and it can send back to Earth images from outer space. Powered by huge solar panels, the reflector of the telescope alone is 2.4m in diameter, and its over-all length is 4.26m.

SKYLAB SPACE STATION

This was the first US space station. It was launched into space in May, 1973, and was built within the empty third-stage fuel tank, nearly 54m long, of a Saturn V rocket. For 171 days it was operated as a space laboratory and observatory. One three-man crew spent 84 days on board. After the last crew completed their mission, Skylab was abandoned. It re-entered the atmosphere and broke up in July 1979.

Index